CHARTS

FOR PIANO SOLO

ISBN 978-1-4950-4595-0

HAL•LEONARD®
CORPORATION

7777 W. BLUEMOUND RD. P.O. BOX 13819 MILWAUKEE, WI 53213

Visit Hal Leonard Online at
www.halleonard.com

CONTENTS

ALL OF ME

Words and Music by JOHN STEPHENS
and TOBY GAD

Moderately slow, in 2

To Coda ⊕

D.S. al Coda

CODA

rit.

AM I WRONG

Words and Music by VINCENT DERY,
NICOLAY SEREBA, WILLIAM WIIK LARSEN
and ABDOULIE JALLOW

Moderately fast

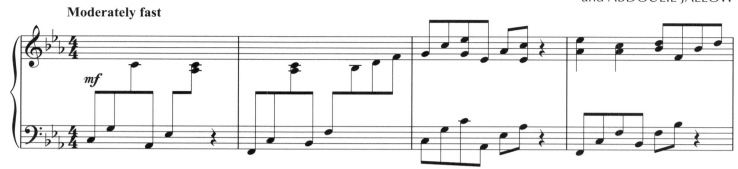

D.S. al Coda

CODA

ALL ABOUT THAT BASS

Words and Music by KEVIN KADISH
and MEGHAN TRAINOR

14

To Coda ⊕

D.S. al Coda

CODA
⊕

CAN'T FEEL MY FACE

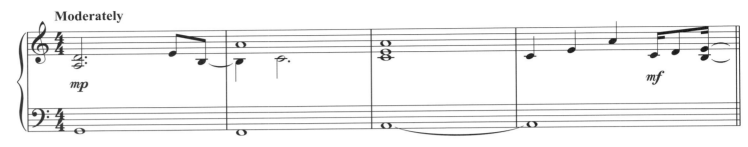

Words and Music by ABEL TESFAYE,
MAX MARTIN, SAVAN KOTECHA,
ALI PAYAMI and PETER SVENSSON

CHEERLEADER

Words and Music by OMAR PASLEY,
MARK BRADFORD, CLIFTON DILLON,
SLY DUNBAR and RYAN DILLON

Moderate Reggae feel

24

LET HER GO

Words and Music by
MICHAEL DAVID ROSENBERG

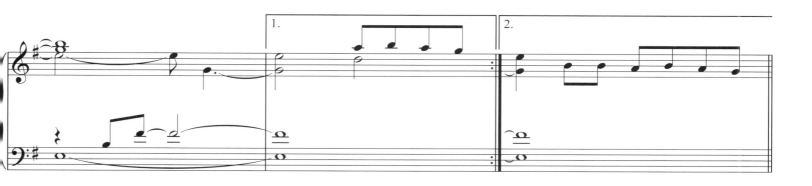

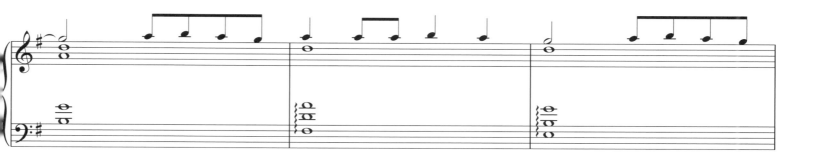

COUNTING STARS

Words and Music by
RYAN TEDDER

LOVE ME LIKE YOU DO
from FIFTY SHADES OF GREY

Words and Music by MAX MARTIN,
SAVAN KOTECHA, ILYA,
ALI PAYAMI and TOVE LO

D.S. al Coda
(with repeat)

CODA

DARK HORSE

Words and Music by KATY PERRY,
JORDAN HOUSTON, LUKASZ GOTTWALD,
SARAH HUDSON, MAX MARTIN
and HENRY WALTER

Moderately fast

LOVE SOMEBODY

Words and Music by ADAM LEVINE,
NATHANIEL MOTTE, RYAN TEDDER
and NOEL ZANCANELLA

RUDE

Words and Music by NASRI ATWEH,
MARK PELLIZZER, ALEX TANAS,
BEN SPIVAK and ADAM MESSINGER

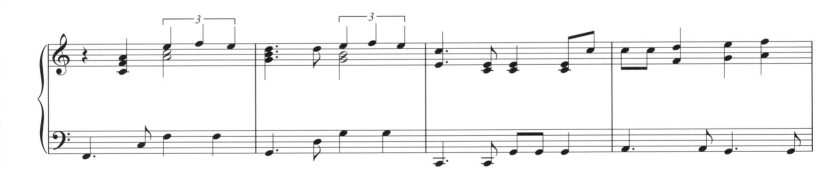

To Coda ⊕

SAY SOMETHING

Words and Music by IAN AXEL,
CHAD VACCARINO and MIKE CAMPBELL

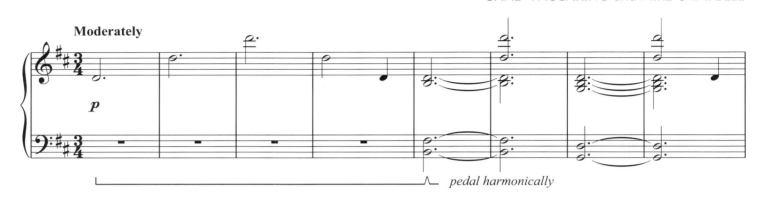

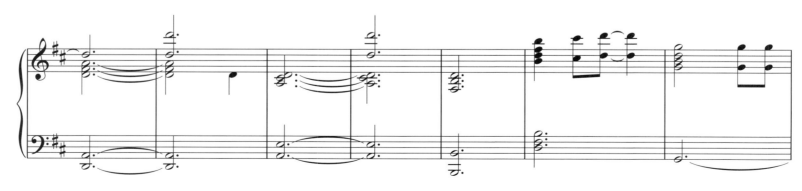

54

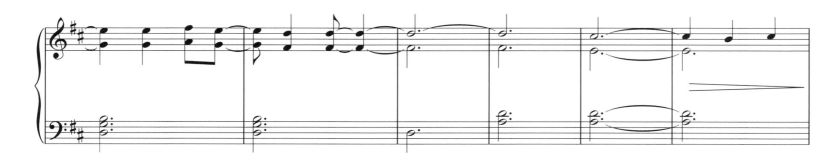

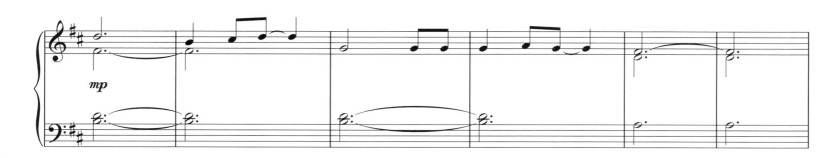

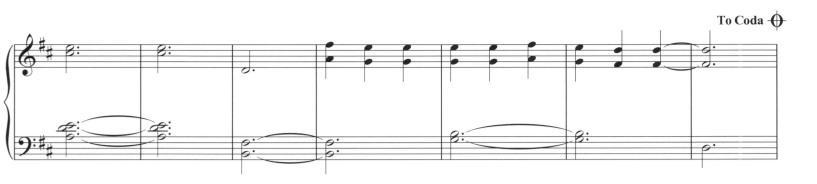

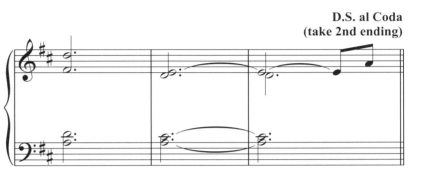

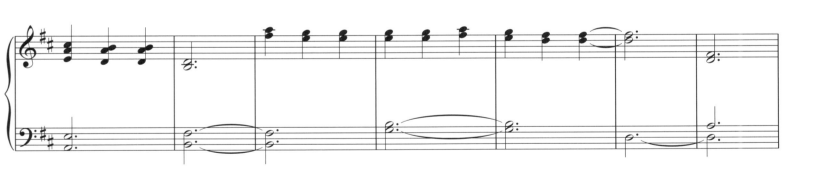

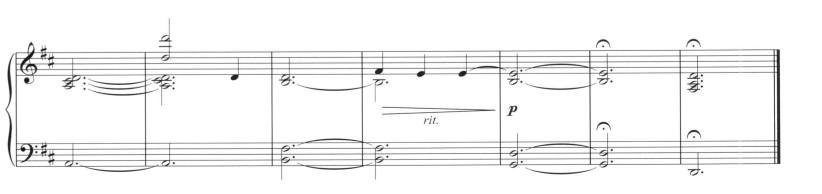

SEE YOU AGAIN
from FURIOUS 7

Words and Music by CAMERON THOMAZ,
CHARLIE PUTH, JUSTIN FRANKS
and ANDREW CEDAR

Soulful Ballad

D.S. al Coda

SHUT UP AND DANCE

Words and Music by RYAN McMAHON,
BEN BERGER, SEAN WAUGAMAN,
ELI MAIMAN, NICHOLAS PETRICCA
and KEVIN RAY

Moderately fast

STAY WITH ME

Words and Music by SAM SMITH,
JAMES NAPIER, WILLIAM EDWARD PHILLIPS,
TOM PETTY and JEFF LYNNE

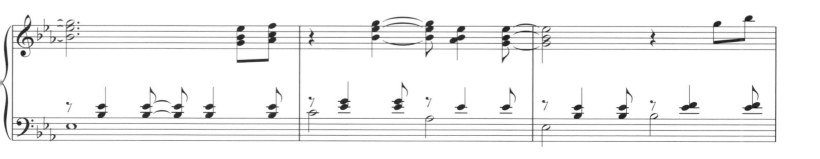

STYLE

Words and Music by TAYLOR SWIFT,
MAX MARTIN, SHELLBACK
and ALI PAYAMI

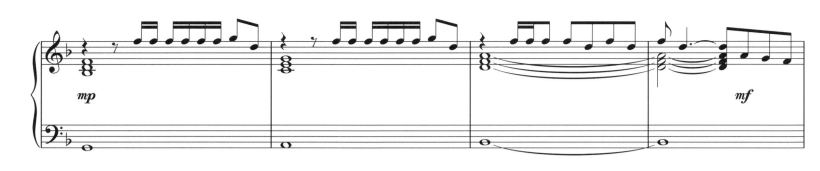

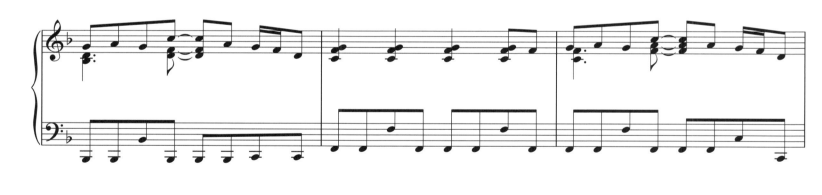

TAKE ME TO CHURCH

Words and Music by
ANDREW HOZIER-BYRNE

THINKING OUT LOUD

Words and Music by ED SHEERAN
and AMY WADGE

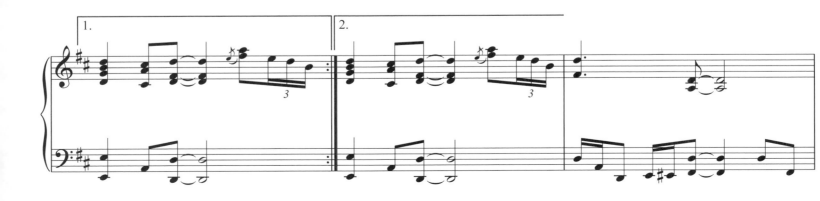

TRY

Words and Music by busbee
and BEN WEST

TEAM

Words and Music by ELLA YELICH-O'CONNOR
and JOEL LITTLE

Moderately

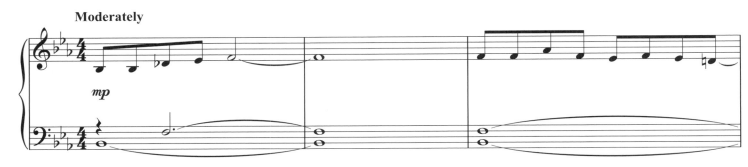

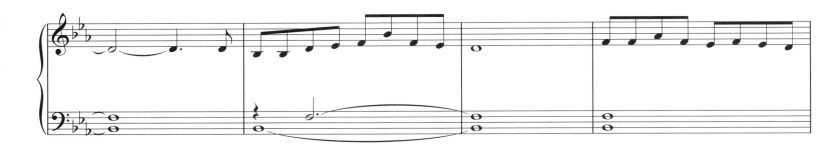

CODA

YOUR FAVORITE MUSIC
ARRANGED FOR PIANO SOLO

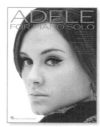

ADELE FOR PIANO SOLO
This collection features 10 Adele favorites beautifully arranged for piano solo, including: Chasing Pavements • Rolling in the Deep • Set Fire to the Rain • Someone like You • Turning Tables • and more.
00307585 ....$12.99

THE HUNGER GAMES
Music by James Newton Howard
Our matching folio to this book-turned-blockbuster features ten piano solo arrangements from the haunting score by James Newton Howard: Katniss Afoot • Reaping Day • The Train • Preparing the Chariots • Horn of Plenty • The Countdown • Healing Katniss • Searching for Peeta • The Cave • Returning Home.
00316688 ....$14.99

BATTLESTAR GALACTICA
by Bear McCreary
For this special collection, McCreary himself has translated the acclaimed orchestral score into fantastic solo piano arrangements at the intermediate to advanced level. Includes 19 selections in all, and as a bonus, simplified versions of "Roslin and Adama" and "Wander My Friends." Contains a note from McCreary, as well as a biography.
00313530 ....$16.99

PRIDE & PREJUDICE
12 piano pieces from the 2006 Oscar-nominated film, including: Another Dance • Darcy's Letter • Georgiana • Leaving Netherfield • Liz on Top of the World • Meryton Townhall • The Secret Life of Daydreams • Stars and Butterflies • and more.
00313327 ....$14.99

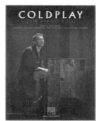

COLDPLAY FOR PIANO SOLO
Stellar solo arrangements of a dozen smash hits from Coldplay: Clocks • Fix You • In My Place • Lost! • Paradise • The Scientist • Speed of Sound • Trouble • Up in Flames • Viva La Vida • What If • Yellow.
00307637 ....$14.99

GEORGE GERSHWIN – RHAPSODY IN BLUE (ORIGINAL)
Alfred Publishing Co.
George Gershwin's own piano solo arrangement of his classic contemporary masterpiece for piano and orchestra. This masterful measure-for-measure two-hand adaptation of the complete modern concerto for piano and orchestra incorporates all orchestral parts and piano passages into two staves while retaining the clarity, sonority, and brilliance of the original.
00321589 ....$16.99

DISNEY SONGS
12 Disney favorites in beautiful piano solo arrangements, including: Bella Notte (This Is the Night) • Can I Have This Dance • Feed the Birds • He's a Tramp • I'm Late • The Medallion Calls • Once Upon a Dream • A Spoonful of Sugar • That's How You Know • We're All in This Together • You Are the Music in Me • You'll Be in My Heart (Pop Version).
00313527 ....$12.99

TAYLOR SWIFT FOR PIANO SOLO
Easy arrangements of 15 of Taylor's biggest hits: Back to December • Fearless • Fifteen • Love Story • Mean • Mine • Our Song • Picture to Burn • Should've Said No • Sparks Fly • Speak Now • The Story of Us • Teardrops on My Guitar • White Horse • You Belong with Me.
00307375 ....$16.99

GLEE
Super solo piano arrangements of 14 tunes featured in *Glee*: As If We Never Said Goodbye • Beautiful • Blackbird • Don't Stop Believin' • Dream On • Fix You • Hello • I Dreamed a Dream • Landslide • Rolling in the Deep • Sway • (I've Had) The Time of My Life • To Sir, With Love • Uptown Girl.
00312654 ....$14.99

TWILIGHT – THE SCORE
by Carter Burwell
Here are piano solo arrangements of music Burwell composed for this film, including the achingly beautiful "Bella's Lullaby" and ten more pieces: Dinner with His Family • Edward at Her Bed • I Dreamt of Edward • I Would Be the Meal • Phascination Phase • Stuck Here like Mom • Tracking • Who Are They? • and more.
00313440 ....$14.99

GREAT PIANO SOLOS
A diverse collection of music designed to give pianists hours of enjoyment. 45 pieces, including: Adagio for Strings • Ain't Misbehavin' • Bluesette • Canon in D • Clair de Lune • Do-Re-Mi • Don't Know Why • The Entertainer • Fur Elise • Have I Told You Lately • Memory • Misty • My Heart Will Go On • My Way • Unchained Melody • Your Song • and more.
00311273 ....$14.95

UP
Music by Michael Giacchino
Piano solo arrangements of 13 pieces from Pixar's mammoth animated hit: Carl Goes Up • It's Just a House • Kevin Beak'n • Married Life • Memories Can Weigh You Down • The Nickel Tour • Paradise Found • The Small Mailman Returns • The Spirit of Adventure • Stuff We Did • We're in the Club Now • and more, plus a special section of full-color artwork from the film!
00313471 ....$14.99

GREAT THEMES FOR PIANO SOLO
Nearly 30 rich arrangements of popular themes from movies and TV shows, including: Bella's Lullaby • Chariots of Fire • Cinema Paradiso • The Godfather (Love Theme) • Hawaii Five-O Theme • Theme from "Jaws" • Theme from "Jurassic Park" • Linus and Lucy • The Pink Panther • Twilight Zone Main Title • and more.
00312102 ....$14.99

HAL•LEONARD®
CORPORATION

7777 W. BLUEMOUND RD. P.O. BOX 13819 MILWAUKEE, WI 53213

www.halleonard.com

0714

THE NEW DECADE SERIES

Books with Online Audio • Arranged for Piano, Voice, and Guitar

The New Decade Series features collections of iconic songs from each decade with great backing tracks so you can play them and sound like a pro. You access the tracks online for streaming or download. **See complete song listings online at www.halleonard.com**

SONGS OF THE 1920s
Ain't Misbehavin' • Baby Face • California, Here I Come • Fascinating Rhythm • I Wanna Be Loved by You • It Had to Be You • Mack the Knife • Ol' Man River • Puttin' on the Ritz • Rhapsody in Blue • Someone to Watch over Me • Tea for Two • Who's Sorry Now • and more.
00137576 P/V/G........................$24.99

SONGS OF THE 1930s
As Time Goes By • Blue Moon • Cheek to Cheek • Embraceable You • A Fine Romance • Georgia on My Mind • I Only Have Eyes for You • The Lady Is a Tramp • On the Sunny Side of the Street • Over the Rainbow • Pennies from Heaven • Stormy Weather (Keeps Rainin' All the Time) • The Way You Look Tonight • and more.
00137579 P/V/G........................$24.99

SONGS OF THE 1940s
At Last • Boogie Woogie Bugle Boy • Don't Get Around Much Anymore • God Bless' the Child • How High the Moon • It Could Happen to You • La Vie En Rose (Take Me to Your Heart Again) • Route 66 • Sentimental Journey • The Trolley Song • You'd Be So Nice to Come Home To • Zip-A-Dee-Doo-Dah • and more.
00137582 P/V/G........................$24.99

SONGS OF THE 1950s
Ain't That a Shame • Be-Bop-A-Lula • Chantilly Lace • Earth Angel • Fever • Great Balls of Fire • Love Me Tender • Mona Lisa • Peggy Sue • Que Sera, Sera (Whatever Will Be, Will Be) • Rock Around the Clock • Sixteen Tons • A Teenager in Love • That'll Be the Day • Unchained Melody • Volare • You Send Me • Your Cheatin' Heart • and more.
00137595 P/V/G........................$24.99

SONGS OF THE 1960s
All You Need Is Love • Beyond the Sea • Born to Be Wild • California Girls • Dancing in the Street • Happy Together • King of the Road • Leaving on a Jet Plane • Louie, Louie • My Generation • Oh, Pretty Woman • Sunshine of Your Love • Under the Boardwalk • You Really Got Me • and more.
00137596 P/V/G $24.99

SONGS OF THE 1970s
ABC • Bridge over Troubled Water • Cat's in the Cradle • Dancing Queen • Free Bird • Goodbye Yellow Brick Road • Hotel California • I Will Survive • Joy to the World • Killing Me Softly with His Song • Layla • Let It Be • Piano Man • The Rainbow Connection • Stairway to Heaven • The Way We Were • Your Song • and more.
00137599 P/V/G $27.99

SONGS OF THE 1980s
Addicted to Love • Beat It • Careless Whisper • Come on Eileen • Don't Stop Believin' • Every Rose Has Its Thorn • Footloose • I Just Called to Say I Love You • Jessie's Girl • Livin' on a Prayer • Saving All My Love for You • Take on Me • Up Where We Belong • The Wind Beneath My Wings • and more.
00137600 P/V/G $27.99

SONGS OF THE 1990s
Angel • Black Velvet • Can You Feel the Love Tonight • (Everything I Do) I Do It for You • Friends in Low Places • Hero • I Will Always Love You • More Than Words • My Heart Will Go On (Love Theme from 'Titanic') • Smells like Teen Spirit • Under the Bridge • Vision of Love • Wonderwall • and more.
00137601 P/V/G $27.99

SONGS OF THE 2000s
Bad Day • Beautiful • Before He Cheats • Chasing Cars • Chasing Pavements • Drops of Jupiter (Tell Me) • Fireflies • Hey There Delilah • How to Save a Life • I Gotta Feeling • I'm Yours • Just Dance • Love Story • 100 Years • Rehab • Unwritten • You Raise Me Up • and more.
00137608 P/V/G $27.99

HAL•LEONARD®
CORPORATION
7777 W. BLUEMOUND RD. P.O. BOX 13819 MILWAUKEE, WI 53213

halleonard.com
Prices, content, and availability subject to change without notice.

0415